Copyright STEMTaught. All rights reserved. No part of this publication may by reproduced or distributed in any form, by any means, graphic, electronic, or mechanical, including photocopying, taping, and recording, or posting electronically in any location, any database or memory device without the prior written consent from STEMTaught.

Subscribing STEMTaught schools and teachers may reproduce and distribute STEMTaught material for use with their students.

The Next Generation Science Standards (NGSS) are reproduced with permission from the Department of Education.

By Talia Allen, Aysha Imtiaz, Jake Hunter, Beth Hunter, Grant Cowell.

The Many Shapes of Land and Water: Pirates Use Maps, and So Do We!

Student Edition

ISBN 978-1-952346-51-4

 **Grade 2**
Next Generation Science

2-ESS2-2 Earth's Systems: Develop a model to represent the shapes and kinds of land and bodies of water in an area.

Explore the Phenomenon!

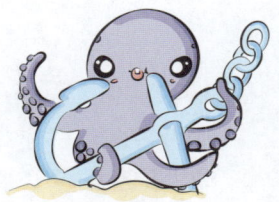

Lesson Anchor

Google Earth Map Scavenger Hunt

Let's go on a trip across the world! Explore Google Earth to search for shapes of land and bodies of water.

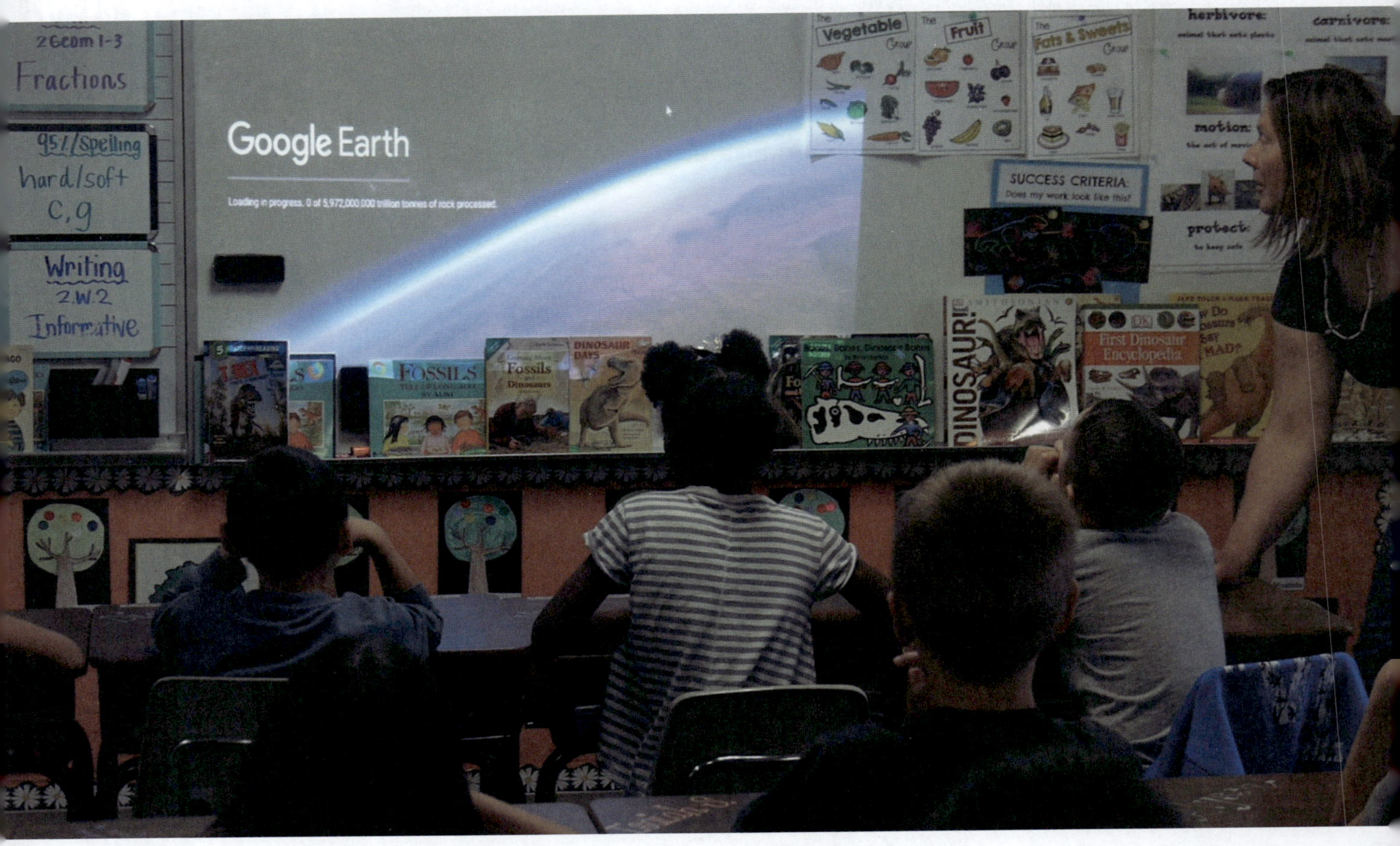

These students explore Google Earth with their teacher.

Open Google Earth:

1. Open "Google Earth." Go to: https://www.google.com/earth/

2. Use your mouse to click and drag to move around the map.

3. Click the "+" and "-" to zoom in and out.

Map Scavenger Hunt

Maps show us features of land and water. Landforms and bodies of water come in all different shapes and sizes.

Explore Google Earth to find the following forms of land and water:

What shape of land is this?

_____

Find a place like this and write its name.

_____

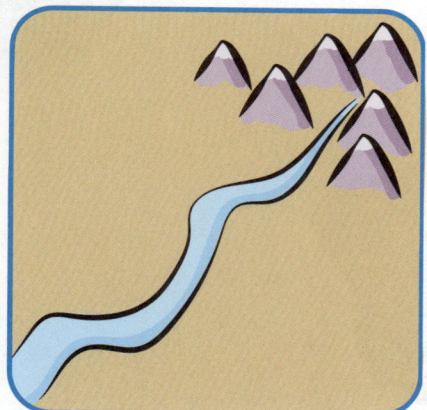

What shape of land is this?

_____

Find a place like this and write its name.

_____

What shape of water is this?

_____

Find a place like this and write its name.

_____

Earth's Continents

The largest pieces of land on Earth are called continents.
There are seven continents.

Label the continents using the clues in the map key.

_____

_____

_____

Draw some sea creatures in the ocean!

_____

_____

_____

_____

Map Key: **The Seven Continents**

North America South America Europe Africa Asia Australia

Antarctica

Land and water have many shapes

When we look at maps, we can see many different shapes of land and water. One piece of land may look long and thin on a map. Others may look fat and round.

Landforms come in many different shapes and sizes! Match the correct tile to the description of a continent.

A Continent

A continent is any of the world's seven largest land masses. The seven continents are: Asia, Africa, North America, South America, Antarctica, Europe and Australia.

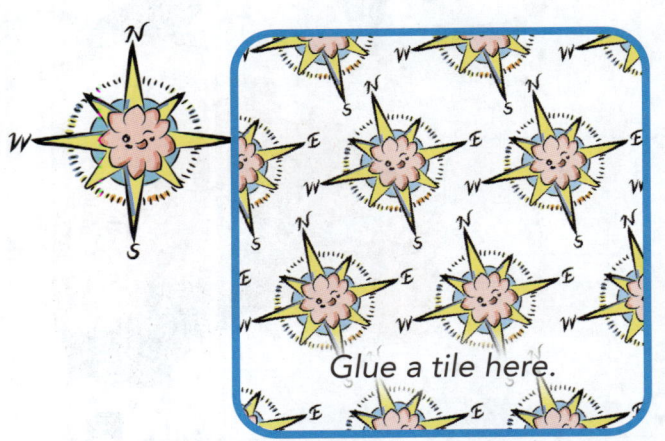

Glue a tile here.

Find the tile that looks most like a continent and glue it here.

I'm going to learn all these landforms!

Practice writing the word **continent**.

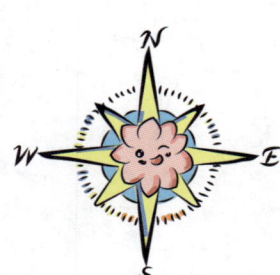

Land Formations

Cut out a tile when you are ready to glue it in its spot.
Match the correct tile to the description of a continent.

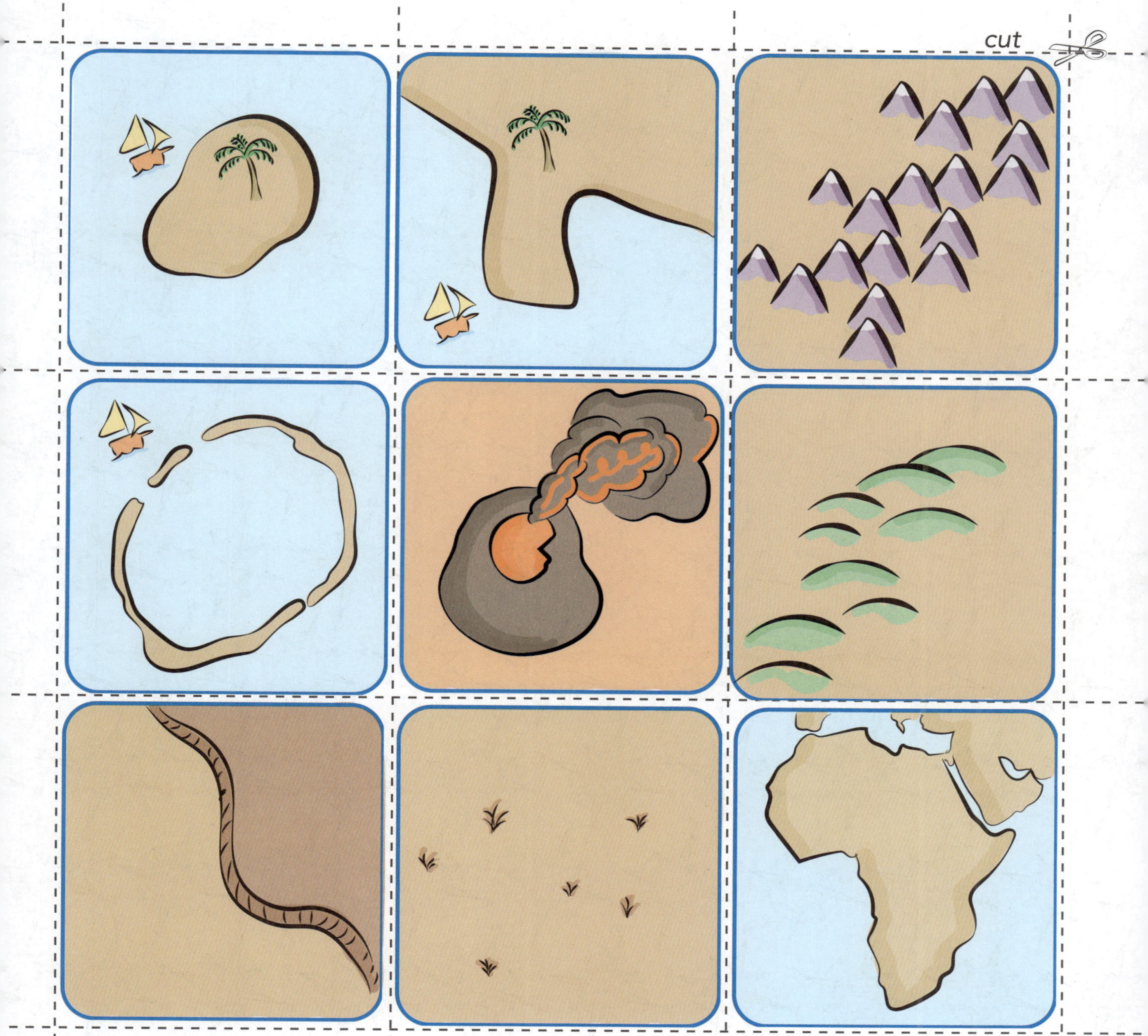

cut

Hill

A <mark>hill</mark> is a round, sloping landform that is higher than flat land. Hills are formed when bits of rock and soil are washed down from taller mountains as they are worn down by water. Hills are fun to sled down when it snows in the winter.

Glue a tile here.

Practice writing the word **hill**.

Map View: Hills look like this from above.

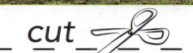

Middle Ridge, Utah

What is taller and steeper than a hill?

I don't know. What is it?

Hills

Want to find a hill in Google Earth?

Try searching:

"Gold Hill, California"

"Apple Hill, California"

"Long Ridge, Utah"

cut ✂

fold

Fold the flap to find the answer.

Mountains

The tallest land formations on Earth are called <mark>mountains</mark>. Mountains are slowly formed when large pieces of land move during earthquakes. Mount Everest, the tallest mountain on Earth, is being pushed up about two millimeters per year.

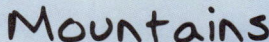
✂ cut

A mountain!

Glue a tile here.

fold

Practice writing the word **mountain**.

Did you know that mountains are found on both land and on the oceans floor?

Mount Everest

Map View: Mountains look like this from above.

Want to find a mountain in Google Earth?

Try searching:

"Mount Everest, Nepal"

"Mount Rainier, WA"

Volcanoes

A **volcano** forms where there is a break in the Earth's crust that allows hot lava, volcanic ash and gas to escape. When a volcano erupts, hot lava cools into solid rock. After millions of years, the cooled lava may become large enough to form a mountain.

Volcanoes form on the ocean floor and on land. Volcanoes can form islands in the sea, mountains on land, and underwater volcanoes.

Glue a tile here.

Practice writing the word **volcano**.

Want to find a volcano in Google Earth?
Try searching:

"Pico Orizaba, Mexico"

"Mount Rainier, WA"

"Mount Erebus, Antarctica"

"Mount St. Helens, WA"

"Mount Nyiragongo, Congo"

"Mount Etna, Italy"

Plains

A <mark>plain</mark> is a low, flat land with few trees. Plains are often covered in grass.

Glue a tile here.

Practice writing the word plain.

What is just as
flat as a plain,
but taller?

Is it an
airplane?

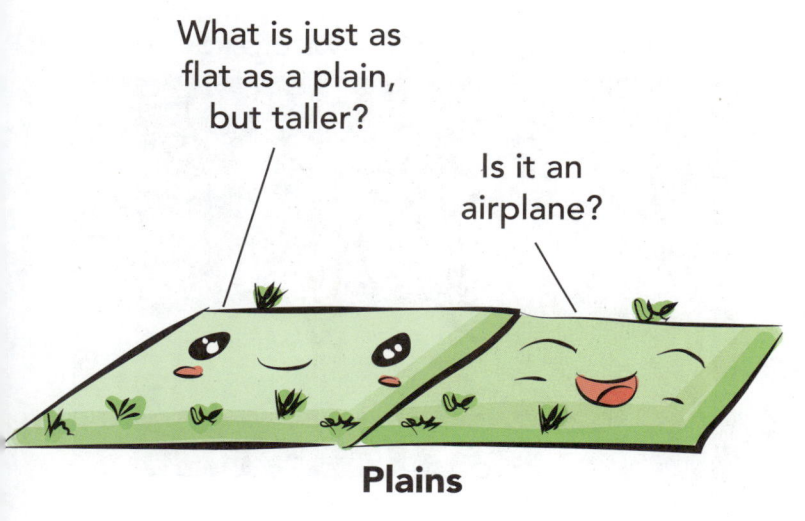

Plains

Want to find plains in Google Earth?

Try searching:

"Serengeti Plain"

"Plains, Kansas"

cut

?

Fold the flap
to find the
answer.

fold

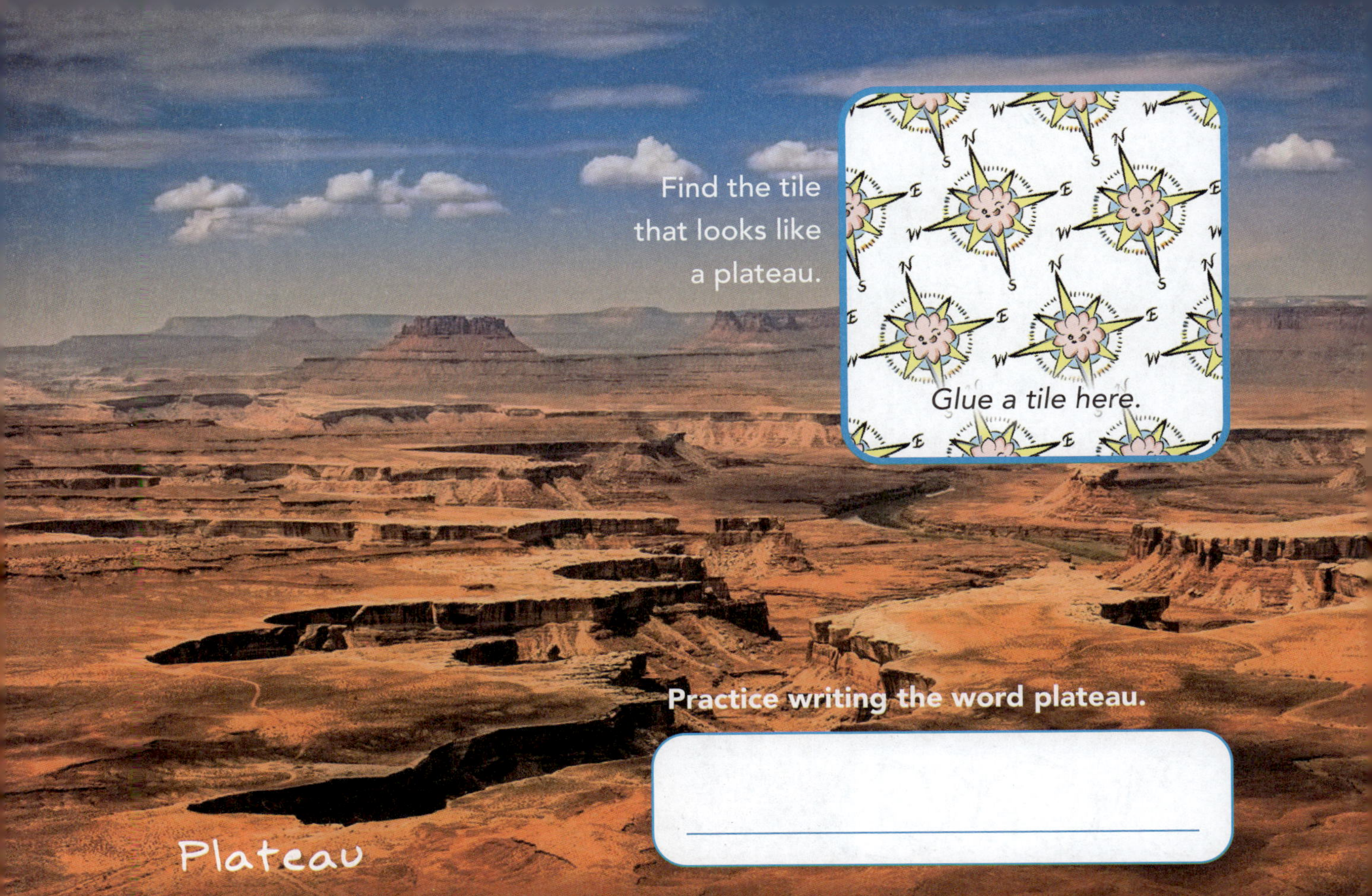

Find the tile that looks like a plateau.

Glue a tile here.

Practice writing the word plateau.

Plateau

A <mark>plateau</mark> is a flat highland. These flat areas are separated from the land below by steep slopes. Plateaus are formed when rivers remove sediment to create low ground next to higher ground.

✂ _cut_

A plateau!

Want to find a plateau in Google Earth?

Try searching:

"Colorado Plateau"

"Muley Point"

fold

Map View: A plateau looks like this from above.

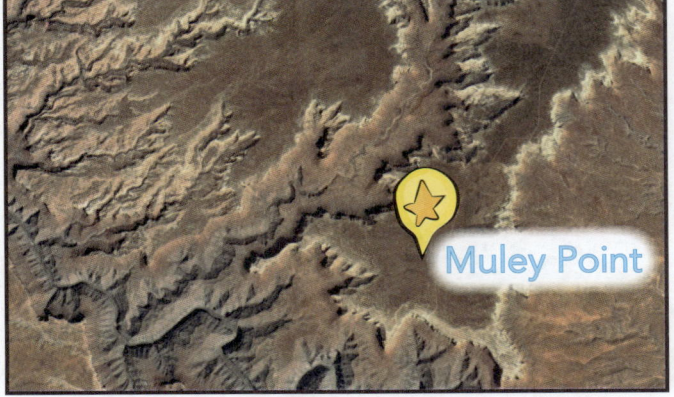

Muley Point

16

Island

An **island** is a piece of land surrounded by water on all sides. Islands are most commonly formed by volcanic eruptions.

Practice writing the word island.

Glue a tile here.

Find the tile that looks like an island.

Today, islands are actively being formed by erupting volcanoes.

What do you call an island with a hole in the middle?

Doughnut island?

Dessert island?

Islands

Want to find an island in Google Earth?

Try searching:

"New Zealand"

"Hawaii"

"Vanuatu"

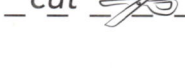 cut

?

Fold the flap to find the answer.

fold

17

Atoll

An atoll is a rare treasure of nature. An  **atoll** is an island shaped like a ring or a donut. It is an island with a hole in the middle.

Practice writing the word **atoll**.

Find the tile that looks like an atoll.

✂ cut

An atoll!

fold

Want to find an atoll in Google Earth?

Try searching:

"Penrhyn atoll"

"Bora"

"Roto"

Volcanic islands commonly sink down over millions of years. An atoll forms when a coral reef grows around and above a sinking island. When an island slowly sinks below the ocean's surface and its reef continues to grow up in its place, an atoll is formed.

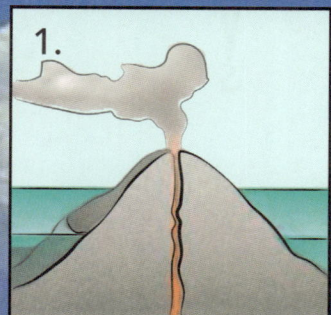

1.

A volcano forms an island.

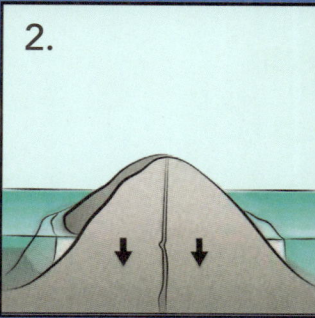

2.

A reef grows around the island as the island sinks.

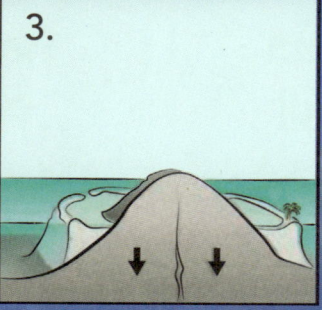

3.

The island sinks more and the reef grows larger.

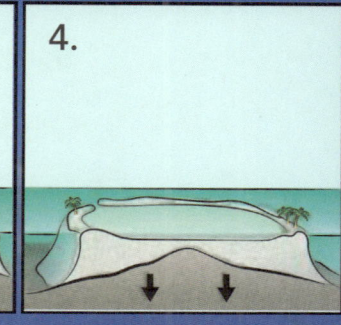

4.

The reef grows up as the island sinks below the surface of the water.

Think, Pair, Share!

An atoll is a very interesting land formation. How do they form?

People live on atolls. Penrhyn Atoll was formed when a volcanic island sunk into the sea. A ring of coral is all that remains of this ancient volcanic island.

Do you know these landforms?

Look at these beautiful photos of Earth's landforms. What are they?

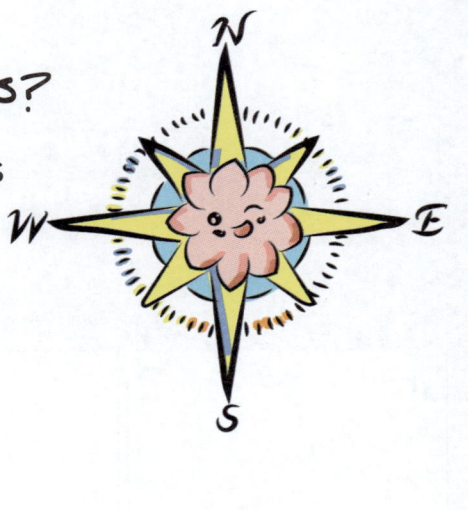

Choose from the following landforms:

Island   Plateau

Atoll   Plain

Peninsula   Mountain   Hill

What landform is this?

_____

What landform is this?

_____

What landform is this?

_____

What landform is this?

_____

What landform is this?

What landform is this?

What landform is this?

What landform is this?

What landform is this?

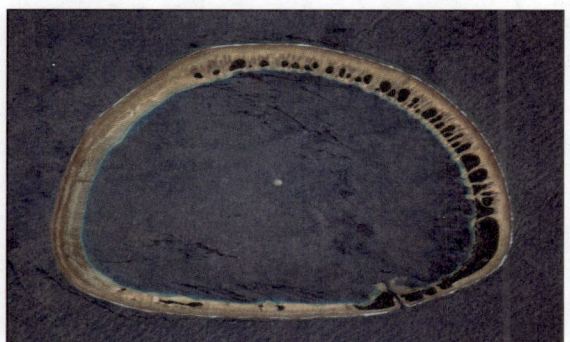

What landform is this?

Map view of Landforms

Can you recognize these landforms in the photos below?

Choose from the following landforms:

Island   **Plateau**

Atoll   **Plain**

Peninsula **Mountain** **Hill**

What landform is this?

What landform is this?

What landform is this?

What landform is this?

22

Bodies of Water

Bodies of water come in many different shapes and sizes! Cut out a tile when you are ready to glue in its spot.

cut ✂

Lakes are my favorite body of water.

23

A lake

A **lake** is a body of water that is completely surrounded by land. Lakes are most often made from fresh water, but they can be salty, too.

Practice writing the word lake.

Glue a tile here.

Find the tile that looks like a lake.

This lake is made from fresh water and is completely surrounded by land.

What is way bigger than a lake and is always salty?

A mountain of potato chips?

Lakes

Want to find an island in Google Earth?

Try searching:

"Lake Powell (UT)"

"Lake Ouler (Ireland)"

"Finger Lakes (NY)"

"Crater Lake (OR)"

cut

?

Fold the flap to find the answer.

fold

Oceans are the largest bodies of water. They cover 71% of the Earth's surface. Oceans are thousands of miles across and separate the continents. They are made of saltwater.

This is a view of an ocean from space.

The water of a salty ocean stretches farther than you can see.

Find the tile that looks like an ocean.

✂ cut

An Ocean!

fold

Find an ocean on a map!

Try searching:

"Pacific Ocean"

"Atlantic Ocean"

"Indian Ocean"

Glue a tile here.

Practice writing the word ocean.

Bay

A 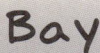 is an inlet of water surrounded by land. A bay can have a small or a large opening, but it is always connected to a larger body of water.

Practice writing the word **bay**.

_____

This photo shows two bays. One bay has a very narrow opening and the other has a very wide opening.

Glue a tile here.

Find the tile that looks like a bay.

Find a bay on a map!

Bays can be huge like the

"Bay of bengal"

Bays can be small like the

"Avalon Bay, CA"

"Monteray Bay"

"Teller Bay, Ak"

27

Find the tile that looks like a river.

Rivers

Rivers are flowing streams of fresh water. Rivers are made when snow or rain comes down from mountains or higher ground. Rivers flow into lakes, oceans or other rivers.

Practice writing the word **river**.

_____

Find an river on a map!

Search "Alsek River," "Coal River," or "Padma River."

Glue a tile here.

Deltas

Deltas form where rivers drain into the ocean. When muddy, brown river water enters the ocean, mud and sediments come to rest and form large piles. In these areas where sand and silt piles up, the river splits up to make fingers that look like branches of a tree.

Find the tile that looks like a delta.

Glue a tile here.

Practice writing the word **delta**.

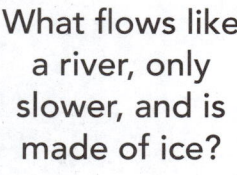

What flows like a river, only slower, and is made of ice?

River

I don't know! What?

Want to find a delta in Google Earth?

Try searching:

"Copper River Delta"

"Bombatoka Bay"

(A delta feeds into Bombatoka Bay)

"Isla Montegue"

 cut

fold

?

Fold the flap to find the answer.

Glaciers

Glaciers are slow moving bodies of ice that form in high, cold mountains and at the Earth's poles. Gravity can cause glacial ice to move or flow downhill. Glaciers can be huge, but they flow very slowly—usually just a few inches per year.

cut

A glacier!

fold

Want to find a glacier
on Google Earth?

Try searching:

"Khumbu Icefall"

"Perito Moreno Glacier"

"Kautz Glacier"

" Margerie Glacier"

Find the tile that
looks like a glacier.

Glue a tile here.

Practice writing the word **glacier**.

What are these bodies of water?

Look at these beautiful photos of bodies of water. What are they?

Choose from the following landforms:

Lake	River
Ocean	Delta
Bay	Glacier

What body of water is this?

_____

What body of water is this?

_____

What body of water is this?

_____

What body of water is this?

_____

What body of water is this?

What body of water is this?

What body of water is this?

What body of water is this?

What body of water is this?

What body of water is this?

Map view of bodies of water

Can you recognize these landforms in the photos below?

Choose from the following landforms:

Lake	River
Ocean	Delta
Bay	Glacier

What body of water is this?

What body of water is this?

What body of water is this?

What body of water is this?

Make salt dough at home (homework)

Make a batch of salt dough and bring it to class with you. You will use the dough to model a map with landforms and bodies of water.

What you'll need to make the dough:

2 cups flour

2 cups salt

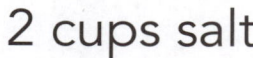

1 cup warm water

Food coloring, paint or watercolors

What you'll do:

1. Mix 2 cups salt and 1 cup warm water.

2. Mix in 2 cups flour with a spoon.

3. Squish and knead until it becomes doughy. Add more flour as needed.

4. Divide the dough into three balls and add green, blue and brown coloring.

Explore
Discover
Excite

Dear Parent or Guardian,

Please make salt dough with your child and send the dough to class with your child in a plastic bag. What will your student be doing with the dough? They will be modeling shapes of land and bodies of water. To represent land and water, your child will need dough of different colors such as blue, green and brown.

How to color the dough:

Step 1: Split the dough ball into a few lumps.

Step 2: Add coloring to the dough balls. You can use craft paints, watercolor paints, Kool-aid or food coloring to color the dough.

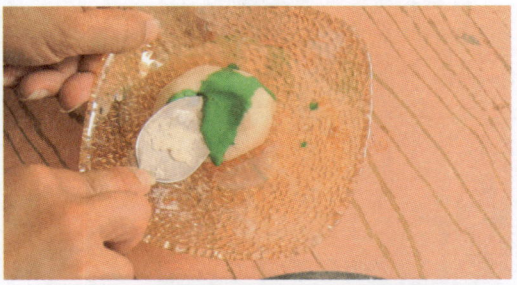

Step 3: Knead the coloring into the dough.

Thank you for making dough with your little scientist.

Sincerely,

Beth and Jake

Model a map with salt dough

Model a landscape from modeling clay or salt dough. Be sure to make different shapes of land and bodies of water.

What you'll need:

- salt dough
- a paper plate

What you'll do:

1. Shape your dough into landforms and bodies of water.

2. Put your land and water features on your paper plate to make a landscape.

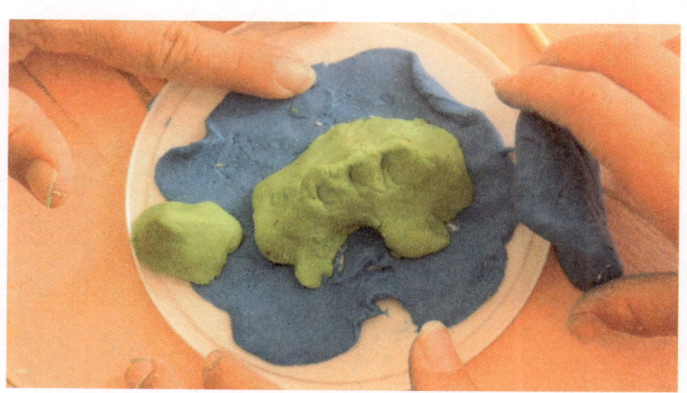

3. Model a pirate treasure chest from dough and hide your treasure somewhere in your landscape.

4. Label your land and water features.

My Pirate Treasure Map

Draw a map of your landscape showing the location of your treasure. Label the landforms and bodies of water on your map.

Lesson Anchor

(Your name here)

_____
Chief map maker

Draw yourself making your landscape.

What is special about your landscape?

_____

_____

_____

What landforms and bodies of water did you include?

Meet the Author

Talia Allen
University of California Santa Barbara
Global Studies

I am fascinated by our world and by people who are different from me. To learn more about people and cultures, I study "Global Studies" at UC Santa Barbara. I learn about languages, cultures, and governments. I often use maps in my studies. I love to travel to new places and experience everything that I learn about. I hope to teach students all over the world.

UC SANTA BARBARA

Listen and **pat your head** when you hear the name of a **landform**.
Rub your tummy when you hear the name of a **body of water**.

Landforms and Bodies of Water

There are oceans and inland seas

We have creeks and rivers that run with ease

Delta waters and lakes so blue

Seas uncharted with islands new

Flat plains, hills and mountains high

Blowing dunes in deserts dry

We've got land and bodies of water

Land and bodies of water

How many times did
you pat your head?

How many times did
you rub your tummy?

Think,
Pair,
Share!

What do a river, a lake and an
ocean look like on a map?

41

PIRATES USE MAPS, AND SO DO WE!

We live on a big planet. Earth is quite large and its surface is covered with oceans and continents.

What continent do you live on?

A long time ago, explorers discovered that there were cities outside of their own.

What city do you live in?

The most curious explorers built sailboats and set out on journeys to travel across the oceans of the Earth.

Draw sea creatures in the ocean.

I am going to tell you a story about pirates who left their island to live on a pirate ship. They used maps every day.

Draw an island in the background.

What island would you want to visit?

Can you help this explorer with her packing list? What is she forgetting? You're right, she's forgetting her map!

Draw what she is forgetting.

But what is a map? A map is something that can show the shapes of Earth's land and water all in one place.

Draw a treasure island on the map.

Draw a volcanic island on the map.

Maps are made to show us where things are. They help us find our way around our big Earth. A map can show just one neighborhood, a country or even the entire world.

One kind of person who uses a map is a pirate. To better understand maps, we will all be pirates today!

The only trick to being a pirate is that you have to learn to say "ARRRRR." So, now everyone knows. On the count of three, everyone say ARRRR!!!

One ... Two ...

... Three!   ARRRRRRRR!!!!

Smart pirates use maps to help
them travel around the world. Here
is ours. Let's open it up!

X marks the spot! When you use a map, it may be helpful to put an X where you're trying to go. For pirates, X marks where the treasure is. Where do you see the X on our map?

Pirates call their friends "Matey". Turn to a friend and say "ARRRR Matey!!" Before the pirates leave, the captain checks his map. They are leaving the land and going out into the sea. To know what way they should travel, the pirates use these directions:

North, East, South and West.

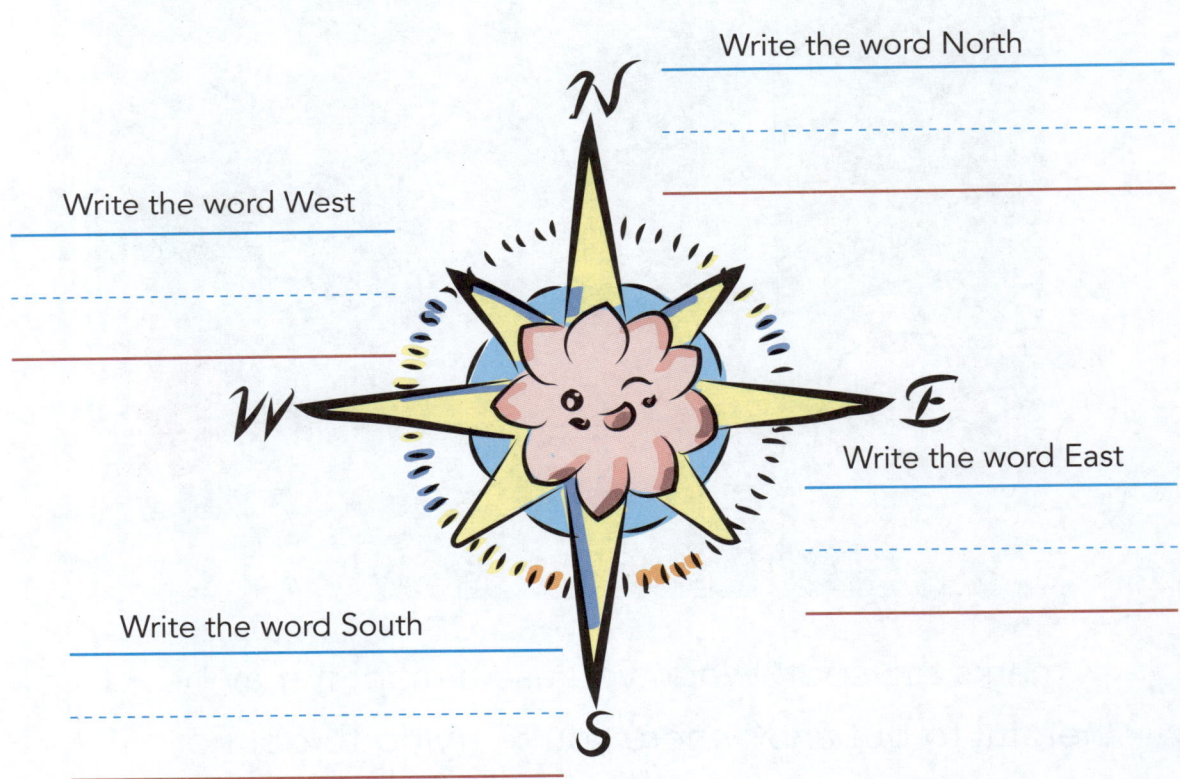

Write the word North

Write the word West

Write the word East

Write the word South

On their journey, the pirates Never Ever Saw Whales. They used this fact to help them remember the directions North, East, South and West because they start with the same letters.

On day 324 out at sea, some pirates get bored. The captain decides to plan a game for everyone to play. He wants it to be a game that the pirates like, so he asks them their favorite sport to play. The options are tennis, baseball, soccer, Frisbee and hockey. He made a chart with the pirates' results.

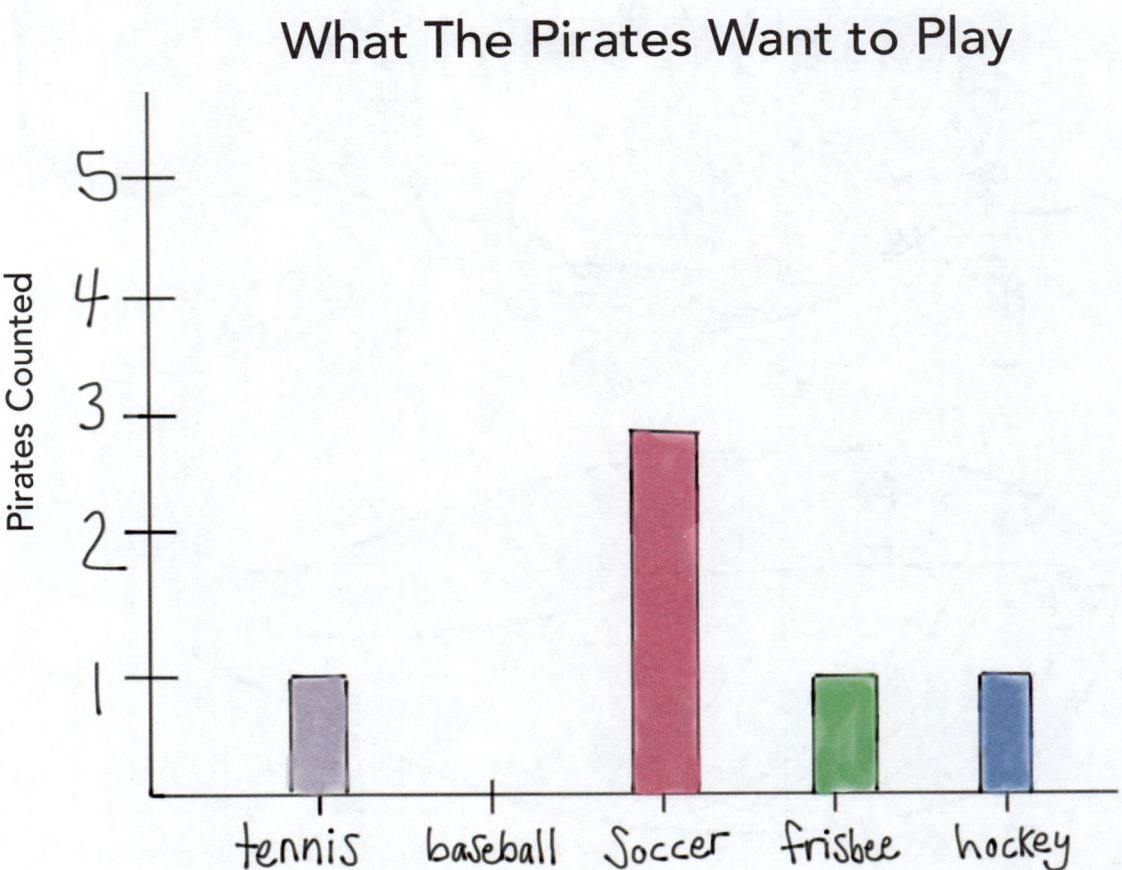

What The Pirates Want to Play

What game do you think the captain will choose to play?

Which game is the least popular?

_____

How many pirates wanted to play tennis, Frisbee and hockey?

_____

Soccer wins the most votes! The pirates play soccer on their pirate ship.

The pirates have so much fun playing soccer! The next week, the captain asks his crew what game they want to play again. All the pirates want to play soccer!

The pirates decide to sail to Argentina to watch a professional soccer game. The pirates use their map to sail south and find Argentina! Their map shows them the shapes and kinds of land and water in their area. Now they can make it to the game!

Which direction do the pirates need to travel to get to Argentina?

_____

Which way should the boat go?

Which way should the ship sail to get to Nessie, the sea monster?

Which way should the ship
sail to get to the turtle?

_____

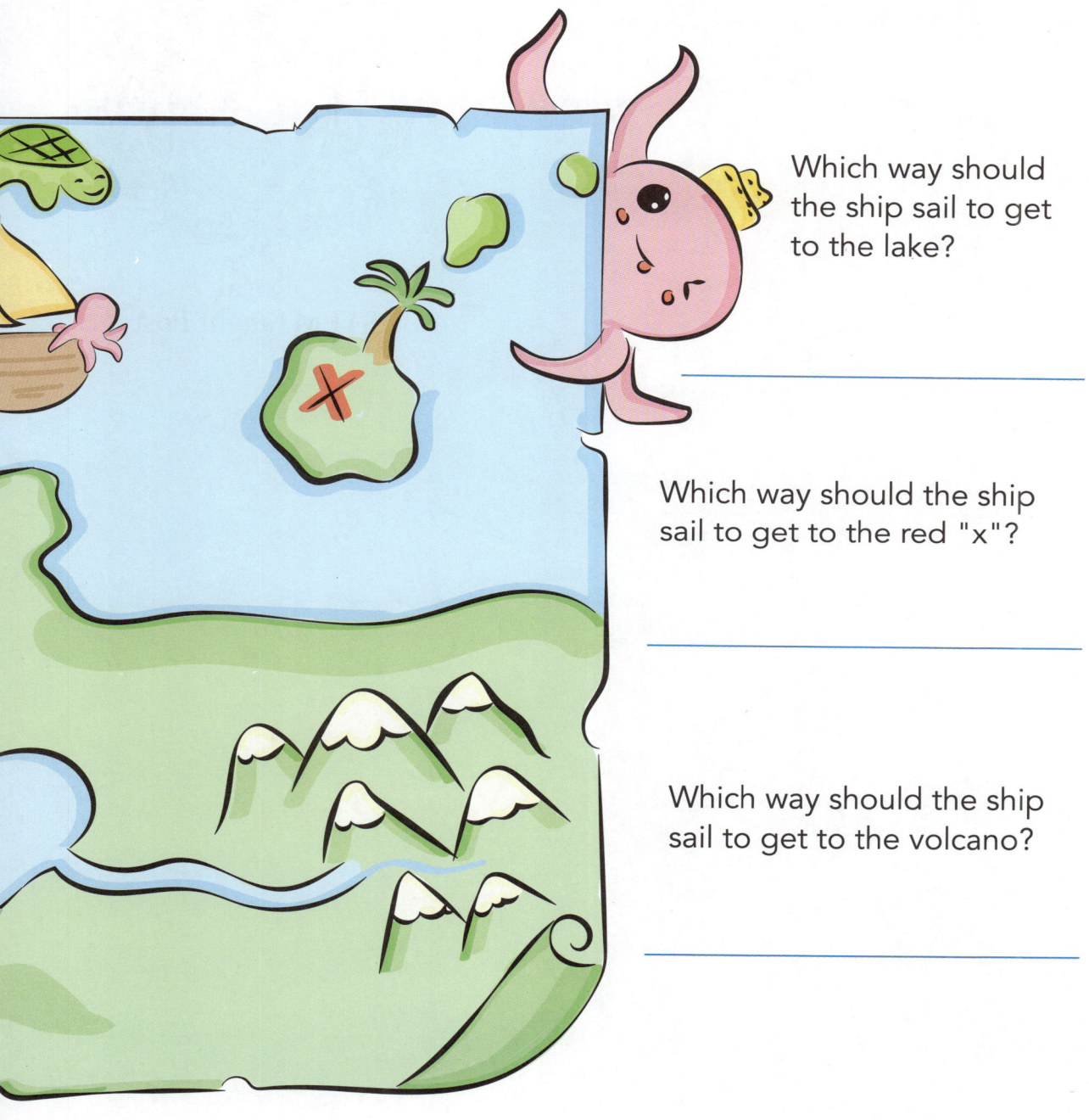

Which way should
the ship sail to get
to the lake?

_____

Which way should the ship
sail to get to the red "x"?

_____

Which way should the ship
sail to get to the volcano?

_____

Which way should the ship sail to get to the mountains?

_____

Fun-Dixie Journal Entry

What was your favorite part of this learning unit?
Draw and write about your experiences.

Official Use Only:

Royal
STEMTaught Post

When you read a great chapter in the STEMTaught Journal and do
the fun activities inside, sometimes you just want to write about it!

Mount St. Helens famously erupted in 1980.

Pico Orizaba, Mexico

There are over 1,500 active volcanoes on Earth today. Humans have observed 500 of those volcanoes erupting.

Map View: Volcanoes look like this from above.

A **peninsula** is land that extends into a body of water. Peninsulas are surrounded by water on three sides.

A peninsula can be as small as a neighborhood or as large as an entire state or country.

Want to find a peninsula in Google Earth?

Try searching:

"Florida"

"Baja, California"

"Italy"

Glue a tile here.

Find the tile that looks most like a peninsula.

The state of Florida is a peninsula, as seen here from space.

Practice writing the word **peninsula**.